Life's Journey:

Love, Life, & Spirituality

A Collection of Poems & Sonnets

by
David Maurice Parker

I0161767

Cover Image © David Maurice Parker

Published by H4TS Media, LLC
                6025 Surrey Square Lane
                District Heights, MD 20747

Printed in the United States of America.
5 4 3 2 1

In Loving Memory:
Mildred Eisbey
Katherine "Grandma Kitty" Robertson
James "Bubba" Mayo

"Happiness lies for those who cry, those who hurt, those who have searched, and those who have tried for only they can appreciate the importance of people who have touched their lives."

- Unknown

"In order to plan your future wisely, it is necessary that you understand and appreciate your past."

- Jo Coudert

Table of Contents

Love .... **Pages 7-23**

    If My Heart Could Talk 8

    I'm Attracted To You 9

    What Do You Want? 10

    I Want To, But Do You 11

    I Don't Want To, But You Want To 12

    The Nature Of My Affection 13-14

    A Letter To A Friend 15-16

    Untitled (You Have My Love) 17

    Untitled (Heart Forecast) 18-19

    A Letter From A Friend 20-21

    The Nature Of My Affection (Revisited) 22-23

Life **24-38**

    When You Leave This World 25

    A Broken Heart 26

    My Friendship With You 27

    Now That You're Gone 28

    Saying Goodbye Is Hard To Do 29

    Have You Ever? 30

    Turmoil 31

    Colors Of Life 32

    Missing You 33

    Apart From You 34

    World's Tragedy 35

    Left To Wonder 36-37

    Positive Destiny 38

Spirituality .... **Pages 39-49**

    Lord, I'm On Bended Knee 40

    Restore My Soul 41-42

Table of Contents (Cont'd)

A Backslider's Prayer 43

The Cornerstone 44

Come, Let Us Worship 45

Praise Him 46

Oh God 47

No Other 48

Renewal 49

God Is In Control 50

LOVE

"If I had a flower for every time I thought of you...I could walk through my garden forever."

- Alfred Tennyson

If My Heart Could Talk

If my heart could talk,
It would say how much I love you,
And why I hold it all inside.

If my heart could talk,
It would tell you my weakness,
And all the secrets I've tried to hide.

If my heart could talk,
It would tell you all the pain I've been through,
And how much I've cried.

If my heart could talk,
It would tell you of all the sadness I've had,
And how much I've tried…
Tried to lock all these emotions inside
In the darkness of my mind,
In the pit of my heart,
And in the depths of my soul
Because I'm afraid…
Afraid of opening up and getting hurt again.
Only, if my heart could talk….

I'm Attracted To You

Your uniqueness attracted me to you
And now I'm deeply in love with you
I'm so in love that my body gets warm while next to you
When I dream at night and daydream, it's all about you

Your humor attracted me to you
I would laugh all day while chillin' with you
When I'm feeling down and hangin' with you
I know you'll say something that'll brighten up my day
Because of the funny things you'll say
That's why your humor attracted me to you

Your intrigue attracted me to you
Your light, intense eyes tells me you have something to hide
Something that you're trying to keep inside
And because of this, I'm attracted to you

What Do You Want?

What do you want?
A romantic dinner
Candlelit for two
We sit across from each other
And with loving eyes,
You look at me and I look at you?

What do you want?
A night full of passion
With us entwined by our legs
We watch the sun rise in the horizon
As we still lay in bed?

What do you want?
Us together in bliss
As we build into a partnership
We share our happiness
And enjoy our relationship

So, what do you want?

I Want To, But Do You

I want to like you,
But do you want to like me

I want to know you more,
But do you want to know more of me

I want to be with you,
But do you want to be with me

I want to love you,
But do you want to love me

I want to give you my all,
But do want to give your all to me

I want to live each moment with you,
But do you want to live each moment with me

I want to be with you forever,
But do you want forever to be with me

'Cause I want to, but do you?

I Don't Want To, But You Want To

I don't want to be with you forever,
But you want forever to be with me

I don't want to live each moment with you,
But you want to live each moment with me

I don't want to give you my all,
But you want to give your all to me

I don't want to love you,
But you want to love me

I don't want to be with you,
But you want to be with me

I don't want to know more of you,
But you want to know more of me

I don't want to like you,
But you want to like me

The Nature Of My Affection

I look at you
And my heart flutters
Your soft, sweet touch
Makes me mutter…
Mutter ooos and aaahs,
Hmms and Mmmms.
Just being around you
Makes me feel good!
Your beautiful smile
And your pretty eyes
With your sense of humor
Sends me to cloud nine!
Your pretty face
And luscious lips
Just looking at you
It's you I want to kiss!
I can't feel this way
'Cause I know you are my friend,
But I would love to be with you
All the way to the end.
To have nights of passion
And days of bliss
Our moments together
I wouldn't resist!

To hold you in my arms,
To have a mutual connection,
And share our deepest feelings
Is the nature of my affection.

A Letter To A Friend

Dear Friend,

We've been good friends for almost a year now, and we've gotten so close so fast. You've been the best friend I ever had and I hope this always last. But, there's something I want to tell you (part of it you already know). So, I decided to write it down and this is how it goes:

I liked you the moment I saw you and wished that you were single. And, when you looked up at me it sent my body a tingle. But, instead of trying to get with you, I settled to be your friend. As time went by, I realized that my feelings for you didn't end.

This may seem to you as a physical attraction or simply just a crush. But, it's far more than that because it gives me such a rush! I feel good when I'm around you; you brighten up my day. You make me smile, you make me laugh in every single way. I can be myself around you; I don't have to lie. I can talk to you about anything, but that's weird because I'm really shy.

I know you don't believe me being shy, but it really is true because you can see my shyness around other people and notice I'm not around you! You make my body shiver and make my heart beat faster. You make my mind quiver and make my feet feel like plaster.

Oh, I really wish I could tell you how I really feel, but I'm so afraid to tell you that my love for you is real. Yes, I'm in love with you; it's finally been revealed! It took a lot to write this down because I couldn't keep it concealed.

I wish we could be together, but I'm probably not your type. I probably don't even come close to your Mr. or Mrs. Right.

You are a very rare and special person who deserves to have true love. I wish that I could be the one to give you that because to me you are a precious dove. You're the twinkle in my eye, every thought in my mind, every beat of my heart, and every minute in time. You're my sun in the sky and my full moon. You're my spring when pretty flowers bloom.

I know this may sound mushy or even pretty lame, but I thought I should let you know and hope you feel the same. But, even though you may not feel the same as I do... I will always have your back and be a friend to you.

So, in closing, I hope you have some insight into how I feel in my heart. You can do what you want with this letter – keep it, burn it up, or tear it apart. But know, that down the road when your relationships don't seem to be what you like, you'll always have someone who will treat you right.

Sincerely,
Your Friend

Untitled (You Have My Love)

You have my love
I gave you my heart
We cherish our moments together
And hope that we never part
I am on your mind
You make me smile
We joke and laugh
And together, we have a good time
My love for you
Makes me feel warm inside
Our passionate lovemaking
Sends me to cloud nine
I am yours
And you are mine
Let's pray that together
Will be a lifetime
You have my love
I gave you my heart
And our love for each other
Will not let us part

Untitled (Heart Forecast)

Mostly cloudy
Gray skies
High is 68 degrees
Low is 35
With showers in the evening
My heart is in turmoil
Being away from you
Missing you
Wishing you were
Here with me…
Holding me…
Kissing me…
Loving me…
Passionately
You in me
And I in you
Sunny
Clear skies
84 degrees
Low 65
Thinking and dreaming
About you
And how things
Will be

When we are
Back in each others arms
Loving freely

A Letter From A Friend

Dear Friend,

I'm writing you to let you know that I liked your letter a lot. So, is that what you have been down and distant about? Honestly, I had no idea you still felt that way... I thought that maybe over time you'd put those feelings away.

To be completely honest with you, it's not much that I do feel the same way. I know it probably wouldn't make sense to you, and you would probably think it's a lie... but I'm afraid. Afraid of hurting you like so many others in my past. The fact that I did them wrong and didn't care is why we didn't last.

If you really knew me and how I use to be, I don't think you would still have these feelings and want to be with me. I know that if we would be together that how you feel and what you've said would be true, but I don't deserve any of it. And, I would be afraid of losing you! On top of it, we're going our separate ways... So, how would "we" work? With all the distance and thing going on in our separate lives... would we grow apart, or even have or take time to talk?

I'm putting this all out in the open with all cards on the table because I really care too much about you for me to be the reason why you would hurt. So, let's get together and sit down to talk. We could really discuss this matter further, and say what's all in our hearts....

Hopefully, we'll come up with something which we both could agree. Keep your head up and stop feeling down… know that I love you just as you love me.

Sincerely
A Friend

The Nature Of My Affection (Revisited)

I look at you
And my heart does a flutter.
Your soft, sweet touch
Makes me mutter.
Mutter ooohhhs and aaahhhs,
Mmmms and hmmms…
Just being around you
Makes me feel good!
Your beautiful smile
And your pretty smile
With your sense of humor
Sends me to cloud nine!
Your gorgeous face
And your luscious lips…
Just looking at you –
It's you I always want to kiss!
I would love to be with you
All the way to the very end.
So, the ball is in your court as to when,
And if, you want this union to begin.
To have nights of passion,
And days of bliss.
Our days together
I wouldn't want to miss!

To hold you in my arms,
To build a mutual connection,
And share our deepest feelings
Will be the nature of my affection.

LIFE

"You only live once, but if you do it right, once is enough."
- Mae West

When You Leave This World
Dedicated To: Katherine "Grandma Kitty" Robertson

When you leave this world,
It would tear me up inside
And for many nights
All I will do is cry…
Cry not because you will go,
But because I really love you so.
The more I even think about it,
The sadder I will get.
But, of all the memories I have –
You, I won't forget!

When you leave this world,
I will be happy inside.
'Cause I know you will be in a better place
Where the curses of this world won't reside.
You will watch over me and live on in my heart.
Then, only then, will you and I never part!
So, in closure I would like to say,
I love you in every single way.
From my very first smile to your very last words,
I will miss you when you leave this world.

A Broken Heart

Life is pale,
I'm sad and blue
Because I'm sitting here
Lost without you.
You had my love,
I gave you my heart.
And, in return, you took it
And tore me apart.
That night you said
You were hanging with friends,
I knew our love
Would come to an end
Because I caught you cheating
While coming in from out of town,
And saw the both of you
In our room messing around!
You got up from the bed
And said, "Let me explain!"
I didn't want to hear it
'Cause I was filled with so much hurt and pain.
You cried and cried
And said that you didn't want to part.
But, I told you to go
And leave me with a broken heart.

My Friendship With You
Dedicated To: Close Friends – Past, Present, & Future

My friendship with you
Has it's highs and lows
Especially the times when
We step on each others toes

My friendship with you
Gets me through the day
Because of those times when
You put a smile on my face

My friendship with you
Helps me through the night
'Cause the things you say
Help me sleep tight

My friendship with you
I will always cherish
And hopefully this relationship
Will continue to flourish
I love the talks I have with you
I like the jokes you have me laughing to
And, when we go our separate ways, I won't forget you
Because I appreciate my friendship with you

Now That You're Gone
Dedicated To: Katherine "Grandma Kitty" Robertson

Now that you're gone,
I don't know what to do.
I just can't imagine
Life here without you.

Now that you're gone,
I'm in so much sorrow and pain.
And, everyday that I'm awake
All I see is rain.

Now that you're gone,
Give me the strength I need to move on.
And, find a place in my heart
That I may not feel so alone
'Cause I will miss you now that you're gone.

Saying Goodbye Is Hard To Do

Saying goodbye is hard to do
Because I'm afraid of moving on without you.

Saying goodbye is hard to do
Because I will miss the talks I've had with you.

Saying goodbye is hard to do
Because you were one of few people I cold talk to

Saying goodbye is hard to do
Because I still want to believe that I can talk to you

Saying goodbye is hard to do
Because it hurts more know that I can't talk to you

And, as time goes by,
saying goodbye is still hard to do

Have You Ever?

Have you ever had a situation
Where you loved someone close to you,
And come to find out
That person loved you too?
But, you didn't become more than friends
Because you both cherished that more.
Add the fact, you were going separate ways
Which pushed that out the door.
You continue to love that person,
And continue to be their friend.
And, promised that you would keep in touch
And see each other again.
Days are spent remembering the old times,
And the nights are spent enjoying the rest of the ride.
Going out and partying like you did before –
Enjoying each other and having the time of your lives!
Now, comes the day you dread –
Wishing it hadn't come and wondering why it came so fast.
You look each other in the eyes, give each other a hug,
And hope what you have will last….

Turmoil

Behind walls of guilt, hurt, shame, and defeat,
I dwell in darkness and I'm always in grief.
I am sad when I'm happy, and angry when I'm mad.
I have no since of humor and don't show when I'm glad.
I have no since of hope and lost all my faith.
I amount to nothing, and I will never be great!
I'm not the best friend and never a good host.
I've pushed everyone away – even those that love me most.
I've lost all for love, and lost love too –
Wish I could love me as much as I love you!
Staying to myself and walking a thin line,
Thinking and wondering why am I still alive –
To endure all this pain and have no relief.
So, leave me alone and let me dwell in my grief!

Colors Of Life

Crimson heart,
Sunset tears,
A turquoise passion
Held in for yours.
Green with envy,
Orange in strife,
And white with fear
That scarred you for life.
A purple sensation,
Brown disaster,
A black depression
Where nothing else mattered.
Yellow courage,
Red with anger
A blue suspense
While in danger.
Gray plagued in disease
Lavender with compassion,
And a cream future
Lurking in the horizon....

Missing You

Missing you
Loving me
Dreaming
And hoping
That we
Will still be
In love…
In love
With each other
Missing your face
Your touch
Your pulse
Can't wait
To have you
Next to me again…
Inside me again
Making passionate love
Wishing and hoping
You were here
With me…
Next to me
Holding you
Loving you
Instead of me
Missing you
Loving me

Apart From You

Apart from you,
I don't know what to do.
I'm lost…
I'm dying…
I'm bored without you.
My days are long,
And the nights are short.
'Cause I'm constantly
Thinking and dreaming
Of you and me
Together in love.
Willingly and passionately…
Wanting and loving
Each other intimately.
Wishing and hoping
For an early return
'Cause being apart
From you so long
Really does hurt.

World's Tragedy

Fields of guilt
Wars on lies
Oceans of shame
Mountains of pride
Shields of courage
Badges of bravery
Weapons of torture
Masked by peace
Streets of confusion
Violence in the air
Businesses stealing
People running scared
Lawmakers treachery
Winds of rage
Seas of jealousy
Entangled in justice

Left To Wonder

Left to wonder
Left in shame
Left to think
Left in pain
Hoping and waiting
For this feeling to pass
Praying and yearning
That this wouldn't be my last
My heart is aching
With guilt written on my face
Standing in the mirror
And staring in disgrace
Contemplating when, and if
I will return to my "self"
'Cause I put "self" on the backburner
And my happiness on the shelf
Left to wonder
No longer am I ashamed
Left to think
And coping with the pain
Hoping and waiting
Know this feeling will pass
I'm praying and yearning
'Cause I know this won't be my last

My heart is mending
There's no guilt on my face
'Cause I'm staring up the heavens
Waiting on mercy and grace

Positive Destiny

My phoenix is rising
From ashes of chaos and confusion
My gifts and talents are soaring
With impenetrable fire
Above the winds of failure and defeat
Bringing to the surface
My hopes and dreams
Toward a positive destiny….

SPIRITUALITY

"Knock, and He'll open the door.
Vanish, and He'll make you shine like the sun.
Fall, and He'll raise you to the heavens.
Become nothing, And He'll turn you into everything."

- Rumi

Lord, I'm On Bended Knee
Inspired by a Sermon

Lord, I come before Your throne
And I will give You all the praise
I will exalt You in all things
And glorify You name always
'Cause you brought me through my troubles
And chastised me when I was wrong
You washed away all of my iniquities
And shield me from all harm
For my sins, You sent down Your Son
To be the ultimate sacrifice
So, here I am on bended knee
And offer you my life

Lord, I'm on bended knee
And I offer You my life
I ask that You dwell in my heart
And take away this strife
Lord, I'm on bended knee
And ask that You come in
To restore my strength and renew my mind
So that I may have peace within

Restore My Soul

Restore my soul

Lord, restore my soul
'Cause I've fallen from Your grace
I've committed many sins
And tried to hide from Your face
I went against Your Word
And betrayed Your Will
In spite of all You've done for me
And knowing how Your love feel

Restore my soul

I'm calling on Your name
And ask that You come in
Dwell in my heart and cleanse my soul
That I may have peace within
Oh Lord, restore my soul
And fill me with Your grace
Give me strength and rebuild my faith
So that I can see Your face

Restore my soul

Restore me
Renew me
Strengthen me
Restore my soul

A Backslider's Prayer

Oh Father, Lord God!
I come to you
On bended knee
As a backslider
With a repentant heart
Wanting to be more like you.
Oh God, my God!
The joy of my heart,
The desire of my soul,
And what would please me most
Is to abide in you.
Oh Lord, my God!
Restore my body,
Renew my mind,
And cleanse my heart –
That I may be
A more usable vessel to you.
Dear God, my Father!
I pray these things
And believe it shall be done
In Jesus' name…Amen!

The Cornerstone
Inspired by the Sermon: "Shout Myself Our Of My Situation:
I Demand An Appointment!!!"

Upon this Stone, He built His tabernacle
On this Rock, I place my feet
That I may not sink in sinking sand
But stand firm and steadfast on solid ground
That He may dwell in me and I in Him
With a renewed mind and a clean heart
Renewed strength and abounding love,
And unwavering faith –
Allowing Him to be "The Cornerstone" in my life

Come, Let Us Worship Him

Inspired by the Bible Lesson: "Kingdom-Abiding Citizens"

Come, let us worship Him
Let us come before the altar
And worship Him in spirit and truth
Bow down before Him
Magnify and glorify His holy name

Come, let us worship Him
Let us come before the altar
And worship His glorious name
Standing in reverence
In the beauty of His presence
Exalting and exhorting His matchless name

Praise Him
Inspired by the Sermon: "I Declare War; I Recover All!!!"

The Lord is righteous
The Lord is awesome
The Lord is magnificent
And greatly to be praised

The Lord is sweet
The Lord is good
The Lord is my Savior
And greatly to be praised

Praise Him
Praise Him
Thank Him for His goodness
And let us praise his name

Oh God
Inspired by the Sermon: "No Pain, No Gain!!!"

Oh God, my Savior
Who guided me on my way
And in the midst of my enemies
Led me to my destiny

Oh God, my Father
Who saved me from my sins
Cleanse me up
And make me whole again

No Other

No other love can compare to You.
No other joy can compare to the things You do!

Lord, you mean more to me than silver and gold –
Your Holy Spirit releases wisdom untold!

You're more precious than anything in the world –
More precious than the most finest pearl!

No other peace will be complete.
You're more than enough and can't be beat!

Renewal

Anoint my head with oil
My cup runneth over for Thee
A sweet smelling savor
No one compare to Thee
May You restore my soul
And lead me to a grace untold
My Father, my God, touch my heart
And please make me whole
Heal my body, renew my mind,
And cleanse my poor soul
So that I may begin to walk
The path that You predestined me for

God Is In Control

The storms may come
The winds may blow
The tides may rise
And you're tossed to and fro
Your faith will be tested
You may feel all alone
The seas may be raging
But know that God is in control

www.ingramcontent.com/pod-product-compliance
Lightning Source LLC
Chambersburg PA
CBHW041801040426
42448CB00001B/2